Catholic Humor

Laughter is the best form of Exorcism

Disclaimer:
Not all of these jokes are considered humorous to
everyone. Please laugh at your own discretion. If you
find it funny, please feel free to share it with your
family, friends and loved ones. Please disregard all
stories that you do not find funny. Laughter may also
hurt your tummy, so try not to laugh too hard.

Table of Contents

Lose the Battle, Win the War

Late one evening, a truck driver stopped by a 24 hour cafe/restaurant to grab a snack. A few moments later, three bikers entered the restaurant and started to pick on him. One of them pour salt over his head. The second one started to drink his coffee. The third started to eat his bacon and eggs.

The truck driver must have been a Christian because he casually got up, went to the cash register and paid for his meal. Then he immediately left.

The three bikers sat down in his booth, laughed out loud and poke fun of him. One of them said: "He's not much of a fighter."

The waiter looked outside the window and said: "He's not much of a driver either. He just ran over three motorcycles."

Catholic Dog

A man went to the priest and shared that his favorite dog (Pug) recently died. The dog was like a family member because he had it for about 20 years.

He said to the priest: "Father, I really love my dog and miss him so much. He was like one of my own child. Can you celebrate a Mass of Christian Burial for my dog."

The priest responded: "I'm so sorry for your loss, sir, but we don't celebrate a Mass for dogs. There's a non-denominational church down the street that may help you with a memorial service for animals. You may want to try the church down the street."

The man responded: "Thank you for your advice, Father. I appreciate your condolences. But do you think they will accept a donation of $10,000 for the service?"

The priest: "Sir, why didn't you tell me your dog was Catholic..."

Valentine's Day

A woman noticed that her marriage was becoming dull and wanted to spice things up. One day she approached her husband and said...

"Honey, I had the strangest dream last night. On Valentine's Day, I received chocolate candies, a diamond necklace, and gold earrings. Honey, what do you think that means?"

The husband responded: "Honey, you'll find out sure enough on Valentine's Day."

Sure enough, on Valentine's Day, she received a package from her husband. She quickly opened the package. Inside was a book.

The book was entitled: "The Meaning of Dreams."

ps. I don't think she cook for him for an entire week. He certainly learned his lesson.

Poker

A group of parishioners got together every Friday evening for a game of Poker (Texas Hold-em).

Bob was an aggressive player that can usually win big but also lose his entire bankroll.

One evening, Bob lost about $1000. He grabbed his chest, and fell over dead.

His buddies wasn't entirely sure what to do, but they knew they had to tell his wife. They went to her and shared the news. With great courage, one of them decided to inform Bob's wife. The others advise him to be gentle. He assured them that he would wisely become the essence of tactfulness.

He went to her house, knock on the door, and said to her: "Your husband just lost $1000 in a poker game, and he can't come home."

She replied: "Tell him to drop dead."

He responded: "Yes, I'll be sure to tell him that."

Walking Out

One Sunday, during the Homily, the priest was so long-winded. A man immediately got up and walked out. He came back just right before Holy Communion.

The priest took the man aside after Mass and asked him: "Sir, I noticed that you got up and left during the homily. Is everything ok? Did you have an emergency? Did I say something that may have offended you?"

The man responded: "I'm so sorry, Father, but I had to go get a haircut..."

The priest asked: "Why didn't you get a haircut before Mass?"

The man responded: "Father, because I didn't need one before Mass."

The Word of God

One Sunday, the priest was giving the homily and two little kids were in the back of the church giggling and disturbing people.

The Priest was very annoyed at their behavior. So when he finished his homily, he said: "There are some of you here who did not hear a word I just said." That quickly quieted them down.

After Mass, three adults approached the priest and said: "Father, we are very sorry, but we fell asleep during the homily. We want to assure you that it will not happen again."

The Shopping Temptation

A Woman went shopping and saw the most beautiful dress that she had to have. Its cost was almost $1000. She charged it to her credit card, and left the store with great joy, excitement and enthusiasm. But she was very reluctant to share the news with her husband, knowing very well that he will scold and shame her for falling into temptation and spending so much money on one dress.

That evening, when she showed her husband the impressive dress, her husband advise her: "Honey, when you are tempted, you have to say like Jesus: "Get behind me, Satan."

She responded: "I did that, but the devil told me that I also look fantastic from behind."

Moses

One day, after faith formation class, a Mother asked her son what they had learned.

He said: "We learned about Moses. God sent Moses to rescue God's people because they were slaves in Egypt. Moses led the people to the Red Sea. Then he had his engineers build a bridge so that all the people can cross the sea. Then he had people place dynamites on the bridge, to prevent the Egyptians from catching up to them. Then they all traveled safely through the desert to the Promised Land."

His mother said: "Are you sure that is what the teacher taught you about Moses?"

The child responded: "Well, not exactly Mother, but if I told you the way the teacher told us, you would never believe it."

The Power of Prayer

In a small town, a bar was being build. Some members of the church who disapprove of alcohol began to pray against the construction of this bar being build in their home town, because they believe that it would cause lots of problems.

Just before the grand opening, the bar was hit by lightning and was burned to the ground.

The bar owner sued the church on the grounds that the church was ultimately responsible for the demise of his building, either through direct or indirect action or means.

The church denied all responsibility for the demise of the bar.

When it came time for judge to make his decision, he said: "I don't know how I'm going to rule on this. It appears that we have a bar owner who believes in the power of prayer, and an entire parish that now does not."

Lion Tamer

A young student was trying to secure a job with the circus. The only available job was being an assistant for a lion tamer.

So the Manager took the young student and introduce him to the head lion tamer. To show her skills, she stepped into the cage, spoke a command to the lion. The lion obeyed her, lay down, rolled over twice and sat on his hind legs to beg for a treat.

The Manager said to the young student: "Well, do you think you'll be able to do that?"

The young student replied: "I'm sure I could, but first you'll have to get that lion out of there."

The Way to Heaven

The legend is told that St. John Vianney, patron saint of parish priests, was assigned to a remote, unknown city called Ars in France. He didn't know the direction there because he didn't have Google Maps. So he told a young shepherd boy: "Show me the way to Ars, and I will show you the way to Heaven."

A similar story is told that a priest was assigned to give a retreat in a parish. But he was unfamiliar to the territory. He wanted to send a few postcards, and asked a young boy to give him directions to the post office.

After giving the directions, the priest invited him to church that evening. "Come to church, and I will show you the way to heaven."

The boy responded: "I don't think I'll be there."

"How come?" The priest asked.

"Because you don't even know your way to the Post Office."

Empty Promises

One day, Bob, a Catholic, who hadn't been practicing his faith, went shopping in a busy outlet mall, but found it very difficult to find a parking space.

So he prayed: "Lord, if you help me find find a parking space, I promise that I will wake up early every Sunday morning to go to church again. I promise that I will contribute to the Church's needs. I promise that I will make generous donations to the poor and needy."

After his prayer, a car pull out giving him a good parking space with a short walking distance to the store.

So Bob prayed again: "Dear God, never mind, I just found one."

To Brag or Not To Brag

Four women got together for lunch and began to brag with one another about their son's accomplishments.

The first one said: "My son is a priest. When he enters a room, people would greet him with joy: "O, Father. They all run to him, hug him and sing his praises.""

The second one said: "That's nothing. My son is an Archbishop. When he enters a room, people would greet him: "O, Your Excellency. He oversees an Archdiocese. They kiss his ring and sing his praises.""

The third one said: "Well, my son is a Cardinal. When he enters a room, people would greet him: "Oh, Your Eminence. He votes for the next pope in the Sistine Chapel.""

The fourth one was quiet for awhile. Then she finally said: "Well, my son is a male stripper. When he enters a room, all the women scream: "O my God...""

Internet

A young seminarian was assigned to Tanzania for a pastoral assignment for an entire year.

This young seminarian was very much into technology. He has a laptop, iPad, iPhone, iPod, etc. He was concerned that they didn't have internet in Tanzania. So he wrote a letter to the Bishop of Tanzania.

"Dear Bishop of Tanzania, I'm very much looking forward to my pastoral assignment. I do have one question. Will I be able to have access to the internet."

A few weeks later, the Bishop of Tanzania responded: "We look forward to having you here in Tanzania for your pastoral assignment. We don't have internet here, but we will make sure that you have a mosquito net."

Attention Grabber

A newly ordained priest was looking forward to the first time celebrating Mass but he was very nervous. He asked the Pastor what he should say for his first homily.

The Pastor suggested: "The first thing you need to do is say something that would immediately grab their attention. For instance, "The best years of my life is in the arms of a woman, who is someone else's wife..."

When he heard that, the young priest was so shocked...

The Pastor continued... "I'm referring to my mother."

The following Sunday, the young priest heeded the advice of the Pastor and begin his sermon in the same manner. "The best years of my life is in the arms of a woman, who is someone else's wife."

But he was so nervous that he forgot to add: "I'm referring to my mother."

God's Rationale

A very religious man, one day, begin to have a serious attack of appendicitis. He was reluctant to go the doctor, but after much convincing from his wife, he finally went to the hospital for the operation.

The operation went smoothly without a hiccup. When the man woke up, he said to the doctor:

"Doctor, when God gave us an appendix, there must be a reason why God place it into our bodies..."

The doctor responded: "God gave you that appendix so that I could put my children through college..."

Bad News

One day, a doctor called his patient and told him:

"I have some bad news and some worse news. The bad news is that you only have 24 hours to live."

The patient said: "What could be worse than that?"

The doctor replied: "I've been trying to reach you since yesterday..."

Vague

Bob told the funeral director that he wanted the best for his Father's funeral, and to spare no expense. After the funeral, the bill was about $10,000. Bob quickly paid the bill.

A month later, another bill arrived for about $75. Bob assumed that it was something that the funeral director must have forgotten to charge, so Bob also paid for that one too.

Another month went by, and Bob received another bill for $75. So he called the Funeral Director to ask about these recurring bills.

The funeral director told him: "You told me to provide the best funeral we could arrange, so I rented a tuxedo for your father."

Happy Thanksgiving

A woman grew up in a household where her parents were vegetarians. So she never saw a piece of meat at the dinner table.

She married a man who loved to eat meat, so she started to eat meat all the time.

On one Thanksgiving Dinner, the husband shared a story to their children about her history as a vegetarian.

"Your Mother didn't know what a turkey was until she met me..."

No Such Thing As a Stupid Question

A Mother shared her experience about her two daughters. One day, as she was preparing dinner for them, they were watching the Christmas story on the television. The younger daughter asked her older sister a question: "What is a virgin?"

The Mother was trying to come up with an answer that would help her daughter to understand. But her five year old daughter quickly answered:

"A virgin is a lady who eats all her vegetables..."

Made in the USA
Middletown, DE
16 February 2022

61344591R00015